Living a Masked Life

Tarralyn Jones

Cover Art & Author Photos:
Keti Bianchi

Edited and proofread:
First Editing - Professional Editing Services

Cover and Interior Layout & Design:
Tarsha L. Campbell

Published by:
DOMINIONHOUSE
Publishing & Design, LLC
P.O. Box 681938 | Orlando, Florida 32868
407.703.4800 phone
www.mydominionhouse.com

The Lord gave the Word: great was the company
of those who published it. (Psalms 68:11)

Dedication

This book is dedicated to the ones that have become complacent about living behind the mask. Knowingly or falling prey to assuming an identity that has you living a life in bondage. I pray in reading this book will involve

self-discovery, breaking strongholds, taking the necessary steps to remove the mask, live a life of freedom, transparency and being the beautiful and authentic you!

"We all have a social mask, right? We put it on,

we go out, put our best foot forward, our best

image. But behind that social mask is

a personal truth, what we really,

really believe about who we are and

what we're capable of."

***

Dr. Phil McGraw

Acknowledgements

First and foremost, all that I've been through, the Lord never left my side. Deuteronomy 31:8 (NIV) ~ *"The Lord himself goes before you and will be with you; he will ever leave you nor forsake you. Do not be afraid; do not be discouraged"*. I thank the Lord Jesus Christ for molding and shaping me into the woman I am today. I've developed into knowing without a shadow of a doubt when you trust the Lord with all your heart not wavering but standing firm in your faith walk despite what it may look like or become, the results are life changing. You will grow stronger in the Lord, your faith will increase, you will have learned to rest in him, and have an everlasting peaceful bond in Jesus Christ.

Genesis 2:24 (KJV) ~ *"Therefore shall a man leave his father and mother, and shall cleave unto his wife: and they shall be one flesh"*. To my husband, my boyfriend, and my chocolate boo we have indeed weathered the storms of life but we were not pulled under instead we kept treading keeping the Lord in the center of our marriage having the power of prayer to sustain and overcome the good, the bad and the ugly. The results, we are overcomers and a billboard how the Lord can make you an example of victories over life challenges with living your best life. Live, Laugh, Love!

Proverbs 22:6 (KJV) ~ *"Train up a child in the way he should go: and when he is old, he will not depart from it"*. To my mother and father who has laid the foundation for our family with the "holiness stance" in our home instilling Christian values, the power of prayer, being grateful, values, integrity, hard work, be a giver and not a taker, strength of a soldier, persistence, humbleness, loving and treating people with kindness. Thank you for being the parents that made me dig deep to rescue who Tarralyn is and who I've become with your unwavering love and support.

Titus 2:3-4 (KJV) ~ *"(3) The aged women likewise, that they be in behavior as becometh holiness not false accusers, not given to much wine, teachers of good things; (4) That they may teach the young women to be sober, to love their husbands, to love their children".* This scripture the apostle Paul talks about the importance of older women helping younger women. To Velma Dennis my spiritual mother who the Lord placed in my life during a time of brokenness, thank you for your continuous prayers, encouragement, pouring into my life, and helping recognize the courage to move forward in my God given gift to use for his glory.

To my siblings who are twins, Tammela Callins and Tarrence Callins who I love so dear for our unique bond and closeness. Although our personalities may differ, the love, strength with incorporating the foundation from our parents has contributed to our relationship remaining and growing stronger in keeping the Lord first in our lives. Thank you for always being there providing your love and support defining this quote: *"Siblings will take different paths and life may separate them. But they will forever be bonded by having begun their journey in the same boat".*

Thank you to my beautiful children Brian, Candace, and Christian Jones my three heartbeats. My love for my children is beyond words. You are amazing and have so much wisdom, refrained from distractions to perfect special talents exemplified in your careers and life that taught me to *"LOVE LIFE"* contributing to my strength in every challenge that was set before me to *"CONQUER"*, *"FLOURISH"* in my

"FAITH WALK", "VICTORIOUS ATTITUDE", "LOVING ME FIRST", "SELF CARE", and "NO LONGER LIVING A MASKED LIFE" STANCE!

Psalms 34:18(KJV)–*"The Lord is close to the brokenhearted and saves those who are crushed in spirit"*. I often think about how the Lord lead our family to a small church in appearance then but large in providing the impactful anointed word of God under the leadership of Bishop Larry E. Perkins with First Lady Hattie Perkins. A visionary that has poured into the lives of many to trust the Lord and stand on his promises. Thank you for your prayers and standing on the word of God while speaking life and breakthrough in my family and others.

"Wearing a mask wears you out. Faking it is fatiguing. The most exhausting activity is pretending to be what you know you aren't."

***

Rick Warren

Endorsement

"Living a Mask Life" is a riveting read by author Tarralyn Jones. The book will take you on a journey throughout her life as a sister, wife, mother and entrepreneur while concealing her truth from the world.

Her faith in God and love of her family helped her navigate her path, overcome difficult trials and tribulations and ultimately made her a walking expression of what she feels in her soul. While reading this book you will be asking yourself am I "Living a Mask Life"

Connie A Mitchell

I'm delighted to write a foreword for my beautiful and talented sister. Tarralyn's experiences has deepen her relationship with Christ and allowed her to find her purpose which is to encourage, pray, minister & be an advocate for hurting women.

Living a Mask Life is an authentic & transparent book that will empower women to live a free spiritual life while unapologetically loving themselves and realizing they can do anything through Christ which strengthened you. A must read!

Tammela Callins

"I have known the author for over 30 years. She is an advocate in her community and the church. Like most women we all wear many hats taking care of our families, the church, businesses and others. Tarralyn is no different, she is a very caring and passionate woman. She gets things done. Many times we bury ourselves helping others while we ourselves are hurting on the inside. "Living a Mask life" will allow the pages to jump from this book into our very beings as we begin to see ourselves and start peeling the layers in our own lives to become the woman God designed us to be."

In HIS Service
Pauline Whetstone

Tarralyn Jones has always been tough, powerful, creative, organized, and a well-put-together woman. As a teenager Tarralyn successfully planned and organized a top-notch fashion show at a well-known hotel, featuring youth from our community, with the support of the late Bishop L. T. Weaver of Greater Faith Temple Church of God in Christ.

Growing up with Tarralyn was never a dull moment. She always exhibited strength and resilience. No matter what, she never let them see her sweat! Never would any of us expect her to have endured the pain, turmoil and extreme personal conflict that almost destroyed her very being.

Knowing Tarralyn as I do, her spiritual foundation and faith in God is how she found her liberation, ability to forgive and love again, and strength to empower others by her testimony! "Living a Mask Life" is not just another memoire; however, it is a beacon to all of those who are "Living a Mask Life".

Congratulations Sister,
Karen Colbert Adams

"I am confident because I can admit who I am,

what I've done, and love myself for

who I've become."

***

#Lifeback

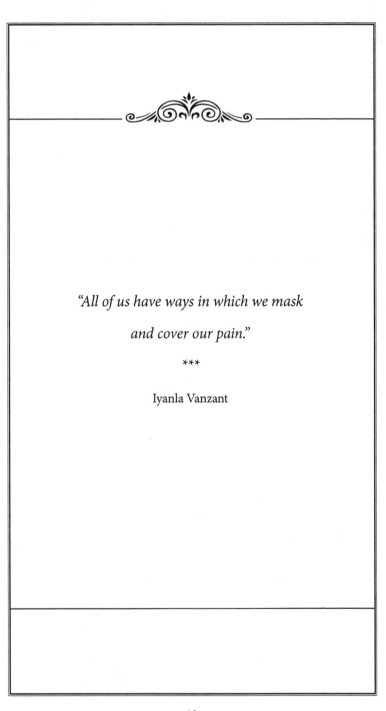

"All of us have ways in which we mask

and cover our pain."

***

Iyanla Vanzant

Table of Content

Table of Content

"*Masking has become a choice to manage disappointment, a toxic habit that has become embedded in your identity. Not recognizing masking causes more harm than good...*"

***

Tarralyn Jones

"You find out in life that people really like you funny. So what do you give 'em? Humor. And then if you show them the other side, they don't like you as much. I find, too, that I can hide behind the idiot's mask being funny, and you never see the sorrow or the pain."

***

Terry Bradshaw

Preface

In today's society, wearing a mask has become the "Norm" in hiding the authentic you and the many things you are experiencing in your life. Before you know it, you've acquired a new identity, "Living A Masked Life."

"As I looked at this woman, I began to tell her she is not the only woman who has or is dealing with turmoil and/or issues in the home. I expressed to her, "You are not alone." There are more women than she would ever know who experienced turmoil in their life while wearing this same mask to simply to cope day to day."

***

Tarralyn Jones

Foreword

Since I was a little girl, I always admired my mother's contribution to women. She'd listen to their stories and create events to bring women together. They would congregate and escape from their quiet sufferings and leave feeling like the strong women they are. They needed a reminder that we all hold stories that are too hard to reveal. So, we sit in our pain and cover it up as a means of survival. The mask we wear builds long time sadness and thoughts of feeling alone in our story. I know my mother's story and had front row seats to years of pain and happiness that would be swept over with setbacks. She'd survive and use it to help other women get up. Her mask was remarkable at times because it gave her the strength to be the face to women trying to stand on their two feet. Her mask was their mask, and her way of keeping herself together was only God. It is an honor being the daughter of someone with a voice to share the stories of the quiet sufferings of women. We must hear it, marinate in it, and continue having conversations as women. May God be with us all.

Candace Jones

"Living A Masked Life" is a real-life story that speaks to a broad audience of women living in disguise - whether single, married with children, sharing joint custody, or executing both roles as a single parent. In this moving and celebratory volume, my mother openly unfolds the courageous story of her veiled days as a devoted wife, mother, sister, daughter and entrepreneur. Her God-given calling to share her testimony on overcoming adversity and self-doubt while enduring a double-masked life of discontentment will have you questioning your own welfare. Are you living your truth? I only hope her story of truth, empowerment, and triumph will grant you the power to release any heavy burdens you may be facing. May your truth set you free and enable you to cross over to a new season of transformation and celebration.

Brian Jones

"Only God Can…turn a mess into a

MESSAGE, a test into a TESTIMONY, a trial

into a TRIUMPH, a victim into a VICTORY!"

***

#Quotesgram

"Personal transparency is the key

to revealing who you really are without the

concern of what others think of you, from

your past to your present. Being transparent

is a form of being genuine, real, and no longer

living in bondage."

***

Tarralyn Jones

Introduction

L iving a masked life comes from suppressing reality—the truth of your personal experiences—and refraining from dealing directly with the issues in your life. Masking has become a choice to manage disappointment, a toxic habit that has become embedded in your identity. Not recognizing masking causes more harm than good; it's only later, when you find out you were masked, that you can see living a suppressed state leaves you living under false pretenses.

Personal transparency is the key to revealing who you really are without the concern of what others think of you, from your past to your present. Being transparent is a form of being genuine, real, and no longer living in bondage. It leads you to an escape route towards living your best life. Living your best life can be defined by this quote by Coco Chanel: "Beauty begins the moment you decide to be yourself."

Dear Heavenly Father, I thank you for giving me the boldness to write this book to connect to those who are living a masked life. As Your sons and daughters read this book, give them the courage, strength, and a deeper desire to have an intimate relationship with you, to lean on and trust in you, Lord. Guide them to no longer living a masked life but instead live their best life, free in living for You with joy and peace.

Let's determine if you are living a masked life. If so, this book will guide you through the necessary steps to remove the mask and begin your path to healing and deliverance.

"I DECLARE I will not just survive; I will prosper despite every difficulty that may come my way. I know every setback is a setup for a comeback. I will not get stagnant, give up on my dreams, or settle where I am. I know one touch of God's favor can change everything. Ready for a year of blessings and a year of thriving! This is my declaration."

***

www.jesuschristislordmdc.net

"Wearing a mask covers your mouth and nose, leaving you to inhale and exhale a limited amount of air; your vision is restricted and your voice are distorted because of the muzzling effect of wearing a mask. The mask is applied only to conceal, to disguise who you really are by stealing your identity and what you are experiencing."

***

Tarralyn Jones

Chapter One

IDENTIFYING THE MASK

Somewhere along the way, you decided to put on a mask, to conceal who you were. The reasons are different for everyone. As such, you must review what triggered your insecurities or your self-blame; what make you want to wear the mask? There could be hundreds of reasons the mask was applied to your face: experiencing years of pain, disappointments, hurts, failures, betrayal, low self-esteem, infidelity, molestation, child abuse, church hurt, or a form of neglect, etc.

Regardless of what pain you suffer through, you should be feeling quite smothered by now. This mask is causing you not to be able to breathe properly. Why? Wearing a mask covers your mouth and nose, leaving you to inhale and exhale a limited amount of air; your vision is restricted and your voice are distorted because of the muzzling effect of wearing a mask. The mask is applied only to conceal, to disguise who you really are by stealing your identity and what you are experiencing.

These are some of the reasons why you feel compelled to wear a mask. But first, let's see the different types of masks—natural and spiritual—to identify if you are wearing one of these masks and why.

The different type of masks are medical, protective, occupational, diving, gas, sports, disguise, punitive, fashion, facial, etc. Let's find out which one you are wearing!

Medical Masks: These are typically worn to protect. Burn masks protect the tissue from contact with other surfaces, face shields protect from bodily fluids, surgical masks protect the surgeon and patient from acquiring infections, and pocket masks safely deliver air during a respiratory or cardiac arrest.

Protective Masks protect the face from a dangerous environment and flying objects.

Occupational Masks are for a profession such as a welding, to protect the face and eyes from sparks and brightness.

Diving Masks are a breathing apparatus.

Gas Masks are worn to prevent the inhalation of airborne toxins and pollutants.

Oxygen Masks are worn to deliver oxygen to the lungs or for pilots that fly at high altitude.

Sports-Related Masks such as a helmet are protective gear to prevent head injuries.

Disguise Masks are worn to not be recognized.

Punitive Masks are worn as a form of humiliation and direct suffering.

Fashion Masks are typically worn as a costume or for a ceremonial function or ritual.

Facial Masks are used for a daily or monthly skincare routine in order to have healthy skin.

Diving Masks are used to see clearly underneath the water.

The question that you are probably asking, "What does the definitions of these masks have to do with me?" I have provided you the definition of various types of masks so you can see the comparison between physical masks and the spiritual ones we wear so you can identify which one relates to you.

For instance, you are wearing the *"Medical Mask"* if you are dealing with deep pains that are embedded in your personality. You are not willing to talk about it but simply avoid the recollection of the events that occurred. You are in need of sensitive care and protection to avoid getting "infected" by negative influences in order for you sustain your health and mental state.

Psalms 13:12(NIV) states: "Hope deferred makes the heart sick, but a longing fulfilled is a tree of life." You must realize everyone has experienced all forms of disappointments or heartbreak that can literally leave behind a heartache that no one could ever imagine. But the God I serve can heal that deep embedded wound you have. You must first comfort your disappointment and heartache, then overcome it. Ephesians 4:31-32 advises us to let go of feelings like bitterness, wrath, and malice and instead be kind, tenderhearted, and forgiving. My God can turn around any situation by administering the right medicine to heal the deep embedded wounds. Isaiah (KJV) 53:5 states, "But he was wounded for our transgressions, he was bruised for our iniquities: the chastisement of our peace was upon him; and with his stripes we are healed."

The *"Protective Mask"* is worn to shield you from dealing with people by becoming isolated. You have set personal boundaries because your trust has been violated in the past; you feel you have to live your life guarded.

There are two scriptures that you must read and absorb their message: (1) Psalms 118:8 (KJV) – "It is better to trust in the Lord than to put confidence in man" and (2) Proverbs 3:5-12

(KJV) – " Trust in the Lord with all thine heart; and lean not unto thine own understanding. In all thy ways acknowledge him, and he shall direct thy paths. Be not wise in thine own eyes: fear the Lord, and depart from evil. It shall be health to thy navel, and marrow to thy bones. Honour the Lord with thy substance, and with the first fruits of all thine increase: So shall thy barns be filled with plenty, and thy presses shall burst out with new wine. My son, despise not the chastening of the Lord; neither be weary of his correction: For whom the Lord loveth he correcteth; even as a father the son in whom he delighteth."

The *"Occupational Mask"* is worn to endure your career path. You have submerged yourself into your career and you have no other meaning in life besides this career. You have failed to include the one important foundation in your success and that is putting the Lord first to direct your path.

Exodus 20:3-5 (KJV) – "Thou shalt have no other gods before me. Thou shalt not make unto thee any graven image, or any likeness of anything that is in heaven above, or that is in the earth beneath, or that is in the water under the earth. Thou shalt not bow down thyself to them, nor serve them: for I the Lord thy God am a jealous God, visiting the iniquity of the fathers upon the children unto the third and fourth generation of them that hate me."

The *"Sports Mask"* is worn to protect you from head injuries. Spiritually, you are suffering silently from a major trauma in your life that may or may not cause you to act out. The suffering includes confusion, disorientation at times, difficulty remembering the past or the present. This mask could be from a person verbally or physically abusing you, or when someone or something just shook you from an unexpected life event. Or perhaps you fell into the wrong hands whether it was trust, marriage, or an event that completely overtook your life. We will not allow this mask to overtake your life. It is time to pray for our Lord to grant you deliverance and victory from the mask.

Romans 10:9-10 – "That if thou shalt confess with thy mouth the Lord Jesus, and shalt believe in thine heart that God hath raised him from the dead, thou shalt be saved."

Psalms 18:17 – "He delivered me from my strong enemy, and from them which hated me: for they were too strong for me."

Psalms 98:1 – "O sing unto the LORD a new song; for he hath done marvelous things: his right hand, and his holy arm, hath gotten him the victory."

The *"Disguise Mask"* is worn so others cannot recognize what you are doing behind the scene. The most dangerous part of this mask you can be standing before a person executing your plans without their knowledge. This mask is unfortunately one of the most dangerous ones. This mask hides envious, gossipers, greed, lust, back-biting, liars, manipulators, etc. If you are battling low self-esteem issues, pride, alcohol/

drug habit, pretending to have it all together, playing a role before your peers/colleagues but really living a false lifestyle, secretly getting close to ones that you are envious of only to destroy them, simply living a life of deceit and corruptness to destroy. Do you recognize this mask? If so, it is time to reveal your identity in order to be delivered and set free.

James 4:7-8 – "Submit yourselves therefore to God. Resist the devil, and he will flee from you. Draw nigh to God, and he will draw nigh to you. Cleanse your hands, ye sinners; and purify your hearts, ye double minded."

Titus 3:5 (KJV) - "Not by works of righteousness which we have done, but according to his mercy he saved us, by the washing of regeneration, and renewing of the Holy Ghost."

Ephesians 6:11 (KJV) - 11 Put on the whole armour of God, that ye may be able to stand against the wiles of the devil."

The *"Punitive Mask"* is worn unwillingly due to humiliation or direct suffering. Typically defined as a form of abuse—sexually, verbally, physically, emotionally, self-neglect, psychological, financially, material exploitation, etc. There are various scenarios of wearing this mask: you experienced being violated sexually, someone constantly verbally abusing you by direct attacks on your self-esteem, someone taking advantage of you by hitting you, you are emotionally drained and withdrawn, you have neglected yourself, or you are emotionally upset and agitated with unusual behavior. You have been taken advantage of financially including illegal or improper use of your personal funds, property or assets. Is this the mask you are wearing?

Isaiah 41:10 (KJV) – "Fear thou not; I am with thee: be not dismayed; for I am thy God: I will strengthen thee; yea I will help thee; yea, I will uphold thee with the right hand of my righteousness.

2 Corinthians 5:17 (KJV) - "Therefore if any man be in Christ, he is a new creature: old things are passed away; behold, all things are become new."

The *"Fashion Mask"* is worn for an event by protocol, or to make a statement to others. Are you wearing this mask to be considered an in-crowd, comfortable doing things others are involved in whether it is right or wrong? Can you be considered a follower with a popular group to gain notoriety? This mask is also worn to simply make a statement, to "keep up with Joneses," by using social media to gain attention of oneself while having a deflated self-esteem. This mask will lead you to a dead-end street named "Void." This street "Void" having you feeling an emptiness in your life. Would you like to know how that void in your life can be filled?

II Corinthians 5:15 (KJV) – "And that he died for all, that they which live should not henceforth live unto themselves, but unto him which died for them, and rose again. This simply means you do not run after what the world does but seek first the kingdom of God and his righteous and all of these things will be added unto you."

Matthews 11:28-30 (KJV) – "28 Come unto me, all ye that labor and are heavy laden, and I will give you rest. 29 Take my yoke upon you, and learn of me; for I am meek and lowly in heart: and ye shall find rest unto your souls. 30 For my yoke is easy, and my burden is light."

The *"Facial Mask"* is designed for daily or monthly skincare routine which involves several methods. Are you the woman who feels your past involves an unforgivable sin? You should not feel that way because you can remove all of that old buildup from the past simply by giving your past to the Lord and asking him to forgive you. Once you ask for forgiveness, all of your sins will be washed away, your whole person no longer being clogged from the filth. You will feel free, pure, and renewed from all of the buildup. If you identify with this mask, it is time to release your sin to the Lord. Your life will forever be replenished from all of the nutrients of what salvation has to offer.

John 8:7 (KJV) – "So when they continued asking him, he lifted up himself, and said unto them, He that is without sin among you, let him first cast a stone at her."

It is time for you to forget the past and not be concerned what others think. Everyone has a form of a past that he or she has been dealing with. Do not allow the devil to hold you hostage. This mask is holding you hostage, let go and let God.

Are you the woman hiding from a deep secret of the past that include molestation, rape, or abuse? It is time to let the past be past. It was not your fault; you just fell prey to the assailant. The assailant will not continue to hold you victim in your mind. It is time to remove the mask so you will not consciously and subconsciously deal with this form of mental attack.

II Corinthians 11:3- (KJV) – "But I fear, lest by any means, as the serpent beguiled Eve through his subtilty, so your minds should be corrupted from the simplicity that is in Christ."

It is time for you to go into a spiritual rehab to release this form of attack in your mind to experience happiness.

Psalms 37:4 (KJV) – "Delight thyself also in the Lord: and he shall give thee the desires of thine heart."

The *"Diving Mask"* is utilized to see clearly under water. The design of the mask is close to your face so it reduces the volume of air inside of the mask so you can see clearer. Are you the woman that feels like you are submerged with issues and problems and can't seem to see clearly without wearing this mask? Spiritually, by wearing this mask, you are not able to see clearly because you are relying on the wrong resources and headed towards destruction.

Proverbs 3: 5-8 (KJV) states, "Trust in the Lord with all your heart and lean not on your own understanding; in all thy ways acknowledge him, and he shall direct your paths. Do not be wise in your own eyes; Fear the Lord and depart from evil. It will be health to your flesh, and strength to your bones." If you just learn to lean or rely on the Lord, he will direct your path with full visibility and clearness. You will be able to see your issues and problems with boldness where the enemy is clearly visible to confront and conqueror.

Remember, without the Lord, your vision will become clouded.

1 Corinthians 13:12 (KJV) – "For now we see through a glass darkly; but then face to face: now I know in part; but then shall I know even as also I am known."

This simply means we only see dimly because our vision is clouded. Sometimes the appearance of things are so limited and clouds our visions.

Isaiah 55:8-9 (KJV) – "For my thoughts are not your thoughts, neither are your ways my ways, saith the Lord. For as the heavens are higher than the earth, so are my ways higher than your ways, and my thoughts than your thoughts."

You may not understand what is occurring in your life; you simply cannot figure it out or concerned if the Lord is hearing your cry. You must exercise your faith and trust that the Lord will come to your aid with clear visibility in your situation.

The "Gas Mask" is worn to prevent inhalation of toxics and pollutants. Are you the woman who is surrounded by a dangerous environment, one where every place you go and every person you know is toxic? In the spiritual realm, you are surrounding yourself with controlling, complaining, negative, unhealthy thoughts and behavior until it is literally sucking the life out of you. This surrounding is exhausting and has become an emotional drain.

You must remove your mask so you can be free from this type of surrounding. As long as you continue to surround yourself with toxic and pollutants it will take root in your life and will be harder to shake or cut them off.

There are many steps to changing your environment, but the first two are:

(1) Read Genesis 39:1- 23 (KJV), a perfect example in the Bible of Joseph and Potiphar's wife – simply cut off the toxic relationship.

(2) Replace your thoughts with God's truths. You must identify the toxic and pollutants thoughts then reject them. Read Romans 12: 1-21, II Corinthians 10:1-6, and Ephesians 6:10-20.

The toxic and pollutants will be replaced with freedom of being delivered with accepting the Lord Jesus Christ as your savior and being victorious. Romans 8:37 (KJV) states, "Nay, in all these things, we are more than conquerors through him that loved us."

1 Corinthians 15:57 (KJV) states, "But thanks be to God, which giveth us the victory through our Lord Jesus Christ."

Finally, Romans 12:2 (KJV) states, "And be not conformed to this world: but be ye transformed by the renewing of your mind, that ye may prove what is that good, and acceptable, and perfect, will of God."

You must know this is not just a physical battle but instead a spiritual battle. Requiring you to summon the Lord's help to lead, guide, and protect you. Are you ready to remove the mask? Hopefully, you are, so you can breathe freely without the fear of inhaling the toxics and pollutants. You will find you are not alone in living behind the mask.

"As she continued to talk and reminiscing on
her life, she recalls masking her life, submerged
in a mental routine of facing reality in fighting
mode. Hiding behind the mask came
from the excitement as a new bride,
setting up her new home
and preparing for her firstborn..."

Chapter Two

The Encounter

Years ago, I had a face-to-face encounter with a young woman. So many of us think only a certain type of person wears a mask, that we can easily spot them in our daily lives. But this woman proves that it can happen to anyone.

She came from humble beginnings, raised in the church, loved to sing, gave her life to Christ at the age of fifteen, and received the Holy Ghost prior to leaving for college. At the revival she went to, she was called out by a Prophetess, who placed hands on her head and prophesied that, "God has His hands on your life and the enemy is going to steal, kill, and destroy you! You are beautiful, vibrant, energetic, full of laughter, vivacious, and God-fearing. The enemy is going to try and take all of that away from you, but he will not succeed."

This happened over thirty-five years ago, but she remembered it like it was yesterday. As she continued to talk and reminiscing on her life, she recalls masking her life, submerged in a mental routine of facing reality in fighting mode. Hiding behind the mask came from the excitement as a new bride, setting up her new home and preparing for her firstborn.

This young woman was already married for two months to a man nine years older than her. She'd met him when he returned to college to complete his degree. But he was secretly hurting emotionally, trying to overcome personal battles and failures on his own with little or no discussion with his wife. These battles involved hidden issues of drug use, unexpected verbal outbursts of rage, and escalating to violence. As she described, if you met him, you would never believe he could ever behave so. He was a hard worker, an excellent coach. Everyone who met him simply loved him. He loved people and would do anything for anybody—a father who loved all of his children and would make every effort to meet their needs. Yet in secret, he fought his demons.

And with those secret demons came a mask for both of them.

"Life is a masquerade. Everywhere you look are

people hiding behind masks."

***

Tarralyn Jones

"To uphold this image, she began to apply the

mask over her face—to deal with her reality,

with the shame of how she allowed this to

happen to herself. This was not

the marriage she envisioned..."

Chapter Three

Applying The Mask

This young vibrant woman was more focused on protecting her husband rather than herself—all to portray an image. While focusing on an image she was also functioning in a combination of fighting for her family and protecting herself from embarrassment, the shame of not seeing the signs early in their relationship. Now she was questioning if she was naïve for refusing to face reality. She put her all into creating this image of perfection—of being married to a handsome 6'4, 250-pound divorcee, an ex-NFL player, and coach.

To uphold this image, she began to apply the mask over her face—to deal with her reality, with the shame of how she allowed this to happen to herself. This was not the marriage she envisioned. The turmoil came from her husband not dealing with the internal pain of feeling like a failure in that phase of his life.

This internal pain caused him to go back to college, to get back on track by completing his bachelor's degree in communications.

Despite this new beginning, he failed to understand he was still dealing with a spiritual stronghold of the mind—a habitual pattern of thought that affected his attitude, emotions, and behavior.

As the face-to-face encounter continued with this young woman sharing her story, Baby #1 arrived, her pride and joy, who instantly made her forget about the disappointments she had experienced, all while hiding behind the mask.

Years have now passed and Baby #2 #3 came along. Her children became her prime focus while she still lived in the shadows of her husband's career, forgetting who she was prior to meeting him. She masked up as the silent mother, continuously praying over her household non-stop—husband and children—forgetting the queen she was.

"She remembered the queen she was and the

game changed."

***

Tarralyn Jones

"She began to look up in the sky and remember

how her husband, little by little, would tell

pieces of his life prior to meeting her, asking for

forgiveness and forever reminding her "you are

too good for me but I love you more than

you will ever know."

Chapter Four

This Means War—Fight For Family

As I looked at this woman, I began to tell her she is not the only woman who has or is dealing with turmoil and/or issues in the home. I expressed to her, "You are not alone." There are more women than she would ever know who experienced turmoil in their life while wearing this same mask to simply to cope day to day. However, as I continued to listen to her, she sternly stated, "We believed in our marriage." She insisted she would fight for her family provided there were no life-threatening occurrences like physical abuse, ignoring that verbal abuse is just as damaging. At this point, she realized this not only a fight but a spiritual warfare. What does this mean?

Ephesians 6:11-12, "11 Put on the whole armour of God, that ye be able to stand against the wiles of the devil. 12 For we wrestle not against flesh and blood, but against principalities, against powers, against the rulers of the darkness of the world, against spiritual wickedness in high places."

She began to look up in the sky and remember how her husband, little by little, would tell pieces of his life prior to meeting her, asking for forgiveness and forever reminding her "you are too good for me but I love you more than you will ever know. I need you in life and I don't know where I would be if you were not in my life."

That was the conversation they both decided to continue and fight for their family and move forward in their life, incorporating the Lord Jesus Christ as the head of their home. As they moved forward, this young woman was so grateful for understanding not only the power of prayer but the use of the scripture, crying out to the Lord for discernment, direction, and providing a sense of peace while going through the storm of life. She saturated herself in the scriptures, not always understanding but always feeling a sense of peace after reading the word. She realized we cannot get caught in what the world thinks because we cannot judge things accurately by our natural eyes; we must have spiritual eyes to see and hear.

The scripture is a spiritual weapon; arm yourself and it will dismantle the attacks of the enemy. If she did not have that spiritual foundation, she would not been able to withstand the wiles of the enemy coming against her and her family. Having a spiritual foundation is understanding (1) Praise and Worship, (2) The Word of God, and (3) Prayer. By putting these three pillars in action, you will experience the powerful presence of God in your life's purpose.

"If you want to put Satan to flight, if you want to get him out of your way – out of your home, out of your family, out of your business rather than just tolerating him and holding off – the weapon you must use is the weapon of attack – the sword of the Spirit which is the Word of God."

***

Derek Prince

"At the age of thirty-five, she found herself

dwelling on these findings. Do I really have

cancer, is this a dream? Why me? My children?

What's going to happen to me?

Am I going to die?"

Chapter Five

First Occurrence

In March of 2002, she remembered feeling some discomfort surrounding a lump in her right breast that caused her to make an appointment with her primary care physician. She felt her schedule was too hectic to accommodate the appointment, but the discomfort concerned her, so she made it work. On April 12, 2002, she received a personal call from her PCP at 4:15 p.m. asking her if she could come to office. She asked why. Her PCP replied, "I have your results from your mammogram and would like to discuss them with you in person."

At that point, she experienced a tightness in her stomach and immediately departed to meet with her PCP. Prior to leaving, she called her mother which immediately began to pray, which provided her comfort while preparing to meet with the PCP. Once she arrived at the office, the PCP greeted her at the front desk and led her to a room to share the results from the mammogram.

The mammogram identified a series of symptoms that indicated breast carcinoma in the right breast. The PCP recommended a consultation with a specialist regarding her right breast carcinoma. While the doctor explained the results, she became weak in her legs but immediately gathered her composure so she could drive home to share the details with her mom, husband, and sister. On May 3, 2002 she had a scheduled consultation with one of the best specialists in Central Florida who scheduled a biopsy. Several days later, the findings confirmed a ductal carcinoma.

At the age of thirty-five, she found herself dwelling on these findings. *Do I really have cancer, is this a dream? Why me? My children? What's going to happen to me? Am I going to die?* Immediately, she changed her mindset and focused on these two scriptures: Isaiah 53:5 – "But he was wounded for our transgressions, he was bruised for our iniquities: the chastisement of our peace was upon him; and with his stripes we are healed," and Psalms 41:3(ESV) – "The Lord will sustains him on his sickbed; in his illness you restore him to full health."

Within the moment internally she was speaking, "I AM HEALED. I will overcome and win."

"You can change the your situation by changing your words… Remember, Proverbs 18:21, 'Death and life are in the power of the tongue, and those who love it will eat of its fruit.' "

***

Tarralyn Jones

"*The first treatment she recalled the feeling like fumes in her mouth and heat going throughout her body later resulting in everything tasting like metal, experiencing nausea, diarrhea, and later lymphedema...*"

Chapter Six

Preparation & Recovery

On May 30, 2002, she underwent a right breast mastectomy with reconstruction. After having surgery, she took her hands and rubbed them across her chest, immediately feeling numb. The surgery entailed removing tissue from her tummy. The tissue from the tummy was used to form a new breast and later another surgery involving a nipple replacement. Now she was focused on taking a leave of absence to concentrate on a series of treatments and recovery.

However, the thought of having the port placement and going through the chemo treatments were horrifying. The port placement was scheduled with the vascular specialist under local anesthesia which was placed under the skin near a large vein in the upper chest where the chemo will be directly delivered into the port rather than the vein, eliminating the need for needle sticks.

Chemotherapy was horrifying to even think about. But luckily, she had one of the best physicians in the country, one known for providing compassionate cutting-edge patient care. Even still, she cried mightily when her oncologist told her she would be undergoing aggressive chemotherapy and lose her hair. She did not accept what the oncologist stated because she had natural thick hair which was her pride and joy. She could not come to grips with losing her hair.

The first treatment she recalled the feeling like fumes in her mouth and heat going throughout her body later resulting in everything tasting like metal, experiencing nausea, diarrhea, and later lymphedema. After going through several treatments, her children, family, and friends could not believe how she was recovering so well and not witnessing any form of setback. She was simply acting normal as if nothing ever occurred. She did lose her hair as the oncologist stated but not her eyelashes nor eyebrows. She was placed on the medicines Adriamycin, Cytoxan, and Tamoxifen. She experienced nausea but no diarrhea and surprisingly returned back to work in her sixth week of medical leave.

Before returning to work she was led to call her insurance company to inquire on wigs for cancer patients. She called the insurance company and found they covered the cost of wigs up to $150. The representative provided her the locations and contact numbers to inquire on the wig(s). After receiving the information, she called immediately and scheduled an appointment. This place was described as the "bomb diggitty," she walks in and pick out the wig closest to her style that she was wearing prior to losing her hair. First, she presented a picture to the consultant then the wig she found in the store. The young lady sat her down in the chair, viewed the pic then placed the wig on her head and customized the wig almost exactly to the style she had always worn. The lady turned the chair around, the reflection in the mirror from the customize wig, she will never forget. As she described, "that lady shaped the wig just like the hairstyle she had worn and no one would ever not know the difference." She remembered as if it was yesterday, she was feeling more confidant as the day was approaching for her to return to work.

"People were observing with some confusion as to why she was not looking or acting like she was undergoing treatment bearing the descriptive names as the non-stop organizer who mastered multi-tasking and doesn't know how to simply 'halt.'"

Chapter Seven

Hurting While Upholding An Image

The day finally arrived returning back to work as the Medical Records Director realizing she truly missed her job, department, friends and especially the owners who she loved so dear. She walks in feeling awkward and out of place to a dead silence room. Everyone turns around and had this confused expression on their faces. It felt like everyone all at once jumped up and started crying expressing how great she looked. Instantly the serious person that she is but sometimes a little silly felt the need to break the tension that was in the room. She can tell no one really knew what to say simply walking on eggshells, so she proceeded to shut the door and told her staff she needed to speak with them. They all turned to face her and immediately she snatched the wig off and she let out the biggest and loudest laughter. She did not know which was funniest the expression on their face or her laughing so hard. Within minutes they were all laughing along with her for several minutes. From that point the atmosphere had changed and the comfort zone restored.

As she shared this story, reminded her of this quote by Betty Wright, "We are stronger than we think and our positive thoughts heal our body." She began to mention the owners of the company that she worked for will forever be in her heart. They stood in the gap for her during the most difficult time of her life. She could never forget how they granted her permission to bring son to work after school and allow him to sit in the back to complete his homework until she was ready to leave. They simply had compassion for her and the children. Not to mention a young man that worked in her department who was tall, polite and considered her adopted son would graciously leave and pick her son up so she could continue to work and bring him back to the office, he will and is forever in her heart as well. Favor! Favor! Favor! As the Medical Records Director, her team became family not to mention the nurses, therapists and all that she came in contact during the course of that time. She continued to work hard but yet kept her mind focused on the healing process while awaiting the results from the treatments. People were observing with some confusion as to why she was not looking or acting like she was undergoing treatment bearing the descriptive names as the non-stop organizer who mastered multi-tasking and doesn't know how to simply "halt."

Finally, the day came for her last treatment and she was tolerating it well. She received the "BIG" news she was "CANCER FREE." Ringing that bell surrounded by her oncologist, nurses, and family was a moment she will never forget. All she could do was raise her arms and holler, "We Serve A Mighty God! Thank You Jesus!"

"God is doing a new thing. He is releasing

healing, forgiveness, joy, peace, victory.

This is your time."

***

Tarralyn Jones

"The sounds of her cry awaken the kids and they all came running in her bedroom. She told them to lay across the bed and she began to tell them what has happened and how they were going to get through this ordeal."

Chapter Eight

Devastation While Hiding
Behind The Mask

Moving forward on the morning of January 10, 2004, she received a devastating call that blind-sided her, leaving her in a weakened state. Realizing the seriousness of the matter left her bearing the weight of raising the children and upholding and maintaining the household for the next three and a half years. *What is happening? Why now? What am I going to do?* The deep cry from her belly and the seconds of fear that tried to penetrate her thought process immediately was blocked by falling on her knees and calling on the Lord. The sounds of her cry awaken the kids and they all came running in her bedroom. She told them to lay across the bed and she began to tell them what has happened and how they were going to get through this ordeal. "I am drying up my tears and you will dry up yours. We are "Victorious" with God on our side we will survive!"

Life had changed overnight. The car had been totaled, so there was no transportation. She had to salvage what she had, not to mention having to sell several valuable items. She remembered while sitting at the table worried about transportation and how she would get her kids to school. That evening her youngest said, "Mom don't worry we will get a car."

Only three weeks later, her parents called. They'd found a car and paid cash for a vehicle. She rented a car and met her parents to pick up the 1998 Oldsmobile Eighty-Eight LD, 4 door sedan. It was an older model vehicle but felt like a show room new vehicle. She drove home in a smooth driving Oldsmobile, kids smiling and momma relieved that they had transportation. One of her kids who loved to sit in the back as if he was being chauffeured, looked at her and said, "See Momma. I told you we were going to get transportation." At that moment they all started giving God the praise as they headed home.

The transportation issue was now resolved and it seemed the enemy was right around the corner, waiting to attack at a rapid speed. As she recalled it was becoming challenging in their dad's/husband absence having to work long hours, attending games, attending award ceremonies meetings, dances, not to mention making sure children had clothes, shoes, food, etc. All while sitting on a board, chairman of an upcoming Gala and the hardest of all having to hold her composure in the midst of performing all of these duties.

"Someday your pain will become

the source of your strength.

Face It.

Brave It.

You will make it."

***

Tarralyn Jones

"...while going through the changes in her life,

she chose to continue to hide behind the mask.

While standing, she found herself becoming

smothered by this mask because she did not feel

comfortable as to who she was and what

she was dealing with..."

Chapter Nine

Broken While Finding Herself

This was a broken woman feeling the Lord had failed and abandoned her. At her lowest, she was seeking a church closest to their home and she remembered a small church in Oviedo where she attended with husband years prior invited by a friend of his, so she decided to return with the kids. As she drove up to the property, she could hardly hold her head up, hiding behind her mask.

As she walked in the sanctuary, she instantly felt the presence of the Lord. After being greeted, she sat behind this older woman who she immediately connected to without uttering a word. This was a seasoned woman that had the presence of God all around her. Her warmth and compassion were automatically felt. She and children sat behind this woman every Sunday. As she continued to reflect with tears rolling down her eyes, she mentioned her mother prayed that she would find someone that she would spiritually connect with and she did. This woman comforted her with the word of God and checked on her at the lowest times and she and her husband holds a special place in their hearts.

The pastor's message that Sunday and every Sunday thereafter immediately fueled her soul giving her life. She began to find her strength and later she and children joined that church becoming active in many areas in the church. She witnessed the children having a safe haven through the love of Bible study and church services refueling them as well. This ministry blessed her household at the most devastating phase of their lives. She recalls name by name every individual who blessed them during this time not knowing she prayed to the Lord to provide and meet every need and the Lord did just that met every need.

She and the children had to deal with questions regarding her husband and their dad. He was absent at many of the most important events, ceremonies, dances, games, etc. She sealed her home in prayer, praying over her children for guidance, protection, wisdom, favor, strength, discernment and prayed to let them crave and have the desire to live for Jesus Christ. Instilling in them to always be humble and not boastful, be a giver and not a taker, be kind and compassionate to others.

Although she had found a place of worship for her family, it was beginning to take a toll on her for fighting the enemy daily, everyday it was something. She had to remind herself you are a "Warrior" and to keep it moving! Ephesians 6:13 (NIV – "Therefore put on the full armor of God, so that when the day of evil comes, you may be able to stand your ground, and after you have done everything, to stand." She became more focused in her relationship with the Lord, the children and their well-being and not herself while being fueled in the word of God that sustained her mind, perseverance to continue and provide a blueprint to guide her through this phase of in life to uphold the role as the wife and mother. However, while going through the changes in her life, she chose to continue to hide behind the mask. While standing, she found herself becoming smothered by this mask because she did not feel comfortable as to who she was and what she was dealing with and more comfortable living a masked life keeping folks out of her business.

One evening when the kids were sleeping, she felt the stress creeping in her thought process overwhelming her with the several obligations that needed to be addressed. Also, she began reflecting on being too trusting, which resulted in making bad decisions and being hurt in the process. As she started naming the individuals and the circumstances that cost her personally causing hurt feelings, embarrassment and loss, the Lord reminded her of the scriptures:

2 Corinthians 12:9 – "And he said unto me, my grace is sufficient for thee: for my strength is made perfect in weakness. Most gladly therefore will I rather glory in my infirmities, that the power of Christ may rest upon me." Simply saying when we feel weak the Lord is powerful."

Ephesians 4:32 (KJV) – "And be kind one to another, tenderhearted, forgiving one another, eve3n as God for Christ's sake hath forgiven you."

Luke 6:37 (KJV) – "Judge not, and ye shall not be judged: condemn not, and ye shall not be condemned: forgive, and ye shall be forgiven."

Behind this mask, she was not only broken but harboring unforgiveness. She knew if you dwell in unforgiveness, grudges filled with resentment, hostility and vengeance and hostility will take root. Medically, this can cause more harm than good to the body. Forgiving will establish healthier relationships, improve your mental health, lower blood pressure, less stress and hostility, not to mention freedom of the mind.

As we continue to sit in silence for a brief moment, a smirk comes across her face, reflecting on the day she surprised the kids after working long hours moving from the apartment to a beautiful home in a well- established neighborhood. The expression on the kids faces was what she needed while hiding behind this mask. This was a rental home and the owners was God sent. He and his daughter were compassionate, kind, considerate, just to name a few. Without being too lengthy this man and his daughter will forever be in their hearts connected to her family later resulting in purchasing this very home.

She continued to share through it all how God surrounded their family with favor. Showing her although she felt alone at times, the Lord is faithful. The enemy is real and fierce. He will not stop at nothing to defeat and destroy you. Although she was in her darkest moments, she kept reminding herself,

God is greater than whatever you are facing, to put on your armor, stay alert, be equipped and stand strong.

During this time, she recalled how the Lord was positioning her and children for greatness through their individual pains. Daughter was extremely talented academically sound, could sing and dance, just a master at everything she put her mind to do. Youngest son was an athletic beast, a natural in sports since 7th grade. She began to share how her oldest son was graduating from high school with honors, editor of chief of the yearbook, receiving the best high school award recognized by Columbia University of Journalism and Journalism student of the year and all his academic accomplishments but how she did not have the resources for him to college. Mom-mode kicked in asking the Lord for guidance by standing on the word of God, Matthew 7:7 (NIV) – "Ask and it shall be given to you; seek and you will find; knock and the door will be opened to you."

With his academic accomplishments, there had to be a scholarship. She and her son started applying to colleges, financial aid, scholarships, etc. Tears began to flow as she shared the recap of the story. Late in the midnight hour God turned things around and worked in their favor. He earned a scholarship that took care of his tuition, room and board, and books. The meal plan was not initially covered but weeks later funds covered the meal plan. He graduated less than four years from University of North Florida, his major: Communication, his minor: Public Relations. Favor! Favor! Give God all the Praise & Honor!

"*Though fatigued, she was fueled by faith,*
and took steps to remove the dreadful mask.
Despite having success, she was feeling
smothered because of suppressed memories. She
hid behind the mask during her life challenges
and talking about them brought the memories
to the forefront."

Chapter Ten

Not Again—Reoccurrence

As women, we get caught up with their children's schedules, making sure they have everything they need, and unintentionally taking the role of being the CEO of your home. And this woman was no different.

One evening, she noticed a discomfort in her left breast. She immediately went in for a mammogram and the results were crushing—abnormal microcalcification. The treatment for the reoccurrence was radiation along with taking the two medications Femora and Zoladex. During this treatment of the reoccurrence, she felt numb and isolated and wanted to be quiet and have that one on one discussion with the Lord.

"Why does this keep happening to me? Okay I am not taking care of myself by running non-stop and adhering to everybody else needs other than myself. Trying to live up to everyone's expectations, always giving even when you had little or no means to give.

She began to notice, you have people that simply don't like you for whatever reason, but if you give them something, the old saying, "they will get and be gone with it." Therefore, keep your circle small with people that have your best interest at heart. Pray with authority and mean business not getting sidetracked by foolishness. She began to tell the Lord I'm going through this in silence, but I am believing you will hold my hands through it all coming out victorious as the evidence we serve a "Mighty God."

The outcome from the series of radiation treatments with her daughter by her side, was successful. Though fatigued, she was fueled by faith, and took steps to remove the dreadful mask. Despite having success, she was feeling smothered because of suppressed memories. She hid behind the mask during her life challenges and talking about them brought the memories to the forefront. She realized she was harboring anger and unforgiveness, which affected her greatly. Medically, it has been proven your body responds to the way you think, feel, or act, giving you conditions such as cancer, high blood pressure, ulcers, heart attacks, and the list continues.

At that point, she realized we all have chapters in our life we would rather keep unpublished. But it was time to shine a light on the suppressed memories so she could breathe again.

"There is no greater agony than bearing an

untold story inside you."

***

Tarralyn Jones

"God promises to repay, you need no collateral.

You only need to believe the promises of God

and live accordingly. God will and is

restoring their lost years."

Chapter Eleven

Removing of Mask While Reunited

One Friday morning in 2008, she received a surprising call that once again knocked the breath out of her. After three and half years of her husband being incarcerated—the result of fighting the inner demons of addiction—they were once again to be united as a family. The news was shared with her kids and they were all feeling the same. However, being reunited felt a little awkward from years apart, but complete, no more hiding behind the mask. The journey they've experienced was quite challenging, an adjustment, life changing but a journey that impacted each one differently turning their pain to their gain. The first night as a family again, they prayed together thanking the Lord for the beginning of restoration. At that point she firmly stated in Romans 5:3-4 (NIV) – "3 Not only so, but we also glory in our sufferings, because we know that sufferings produces 4 perseverance, character; and character, hope."

Second, she prayed for restoration, Joel 2:25 ~ (25) "I will repay you for the years the locusts have eaten – the great locust and the young locust, and the other locusts and the locust swarm – my great army that I sent among you." God promises to repay, you need no collateral. You only need to believe the promises of God and live accordingly. God will and is restoring their lost years.

"Whenever God restores something, He restores

it to a place greater than it was before."

***

Tarralyn Jones

"While preparing for the surgery, the medical staff informed her family that they were not sure if she would be the same after the surgery."

Chapter Twelve

Equipped & Ready—Brain Tumors

November 21, 2014, she started experiencing severe piercing migraines while driving. They were so bad in fact, she was disoriented and got lost on her way home. After calling her husband and sister, she ended up recognizing Highway 520 and managed to find her way home. Once she arrived home, she recalled seeing her husband and sister standing in the driveway near the garage.

When she pulled up to the garage, she could not recall how to place the car in park. Her husband reached in the car and placed the car in park and helped her out of the car, as she felt dizzy and off balance.

Despite her protestations, they ignored her stubbornness and took her to the emergency room for right side weakness and severe headaches. Once they arrived to the emergency room, the staff immediately took her back and an MRI was performed.

They found a large right parietal lesion and a second lesion, much smaller, in the left hemisphere. The diagnosis (1) to (2) brain tumor right parietal resection: metastic high grade incarcinoma with features consistent with mammary ductal carcinoma. She was transformed to the main hospital campus to prepare for emergency surgery.

While preparing for the surgery, the medical staff informed her family that they were not sure if she would be the same after the surgery. She was told by her mother there were some praying saints in that room prior to going into surgery. Though she doesn't recall much of being prepped for surgery, but vaguely remember seeing her husband, mom, children, Mother/Deacon of church, sister and her pastor, but she didn't see her dad.

She asked, "Where is my daddy?" He stepped forward so she could see him and she felt at ease. Someone in the room said, "She is the spoiled one, daddy's girl." Her mother replied, "Yes she is."

The pastor laid across the foot of her bed while the saints surrounded him and her calling out the name of Jesus. "You are healed! This surgery will have a successful outcome. You have work to do for his kingdom! You will live and not die!"

She felt the anointing flowing from the crown of her head to the sole of her feet. Matthew 18:18-20 – "POWER OF PRAYER" – "Truly, I say to you, whatever you loose on earth shall be loosed in heaven. Again, I say to you, if two of you agree on earth about anything they ask, it will be done for them by my Father in heaven."

The surgery was two hours long and the family was waiting anxiously for an update from the surgery. Finally, the surgeon appeared and said, "Well both of her hands and feet are moving.

Her husband hollered out, "Thank You Jesus. Praising God," jumping around in the room while the others joined in praising God.

That next day, she was laying in the bed asking for her iPad, making demands, checking her calendar while staring at the television. A few minutes later, two therapists started asking her a series of questions, which she answered comically without hesitation. The therapists now wanted to check her mobility, social skills, and cognitive changes. She was reacting so fast, the therapist pushed back, asking her to use a walker.

But she would have none of it, saying she could walk just fine. "Hallelujah, look at me! Who wouldn't want to serve a God like this?" She walked back to her bed with her hands raised, her eyes fixated on the television while the sounds of cheers from everyone in the room watching the football game. In the midst of the cheers from people watching the game, she overheard someone say she is a miracle and she is something else just look her.

All of a sudden, she said, "Hey turn up the television." She began trying to pull herself up while her husband came over to assist her. While she was listening, she recognized her son's name called from the announcer. Her son had a fumble recovery in the third quarter against the Bucs. While he was celebrating his recovery, she was celebrating her recovery as well. She hollers out, 'THAT'S MY BOY! THAT'S WHAT I AM TALKING ABOUT! While listening to the announcer with the tears flowing down her face and to see her son's fumble recovery one day after surgery. This is not a coincidence; this is all in God's plan.

Living behind a mask can easily become a part of your life. In her case, the foundation that was instilled since childhood sustained her through the process being equipped for the unexpected things in what we call "life." We all have a story, no one can dare be judgmental. Because if surveillance was placed on you behind closed doors, I am sure we would find you too are wearing and/or hiding behind a mask. In her case, she chose to tell her story and other cases some feel compelled to continue living behind the mask. Through this process she validated being a wise and virtuous woman defined in Proverbs 14 and Proverbs 31.

Yes, her marriage went through the good, the bad, and the ugly and definitely not the first one that has had this type of journey. Yes there was indeed turmoil, medical challenges, personal pain, losses, and brokenness. You see marriage is a sacred lifelong union and commitment. Mark 10:6-8 (NIV) says, "6 But at the beginning of creation God made male and female. 7 For this reason, a man will leave his father and mother and be united to his wife, 8 and the two will become one flesh. So they are no longer two but one flesh."

Some have forgotten what their vows say and mean; she didn't and neither did her husband. Being happy doesn't mean everything is perfect. It means you've decided to look beyond the imperfection and find the diamond in the rough. Yes, he was a serious personal project, but guess what—he is a diamond in the rough.

Just in case you need a reminder of what the wedding vows say, here it is: "I _____, take you _____, to be my wife (or husband), to have and to hold from this day forward, for better, for worse, for richer, for poorer, in sickness and in health, to love and to cherish, till death us do part, according to God's holy law, and this is my solemn vow."

This face-to-face encounter was me, Tarralyn Jones, having an encounter with myself while taking the necessary steps in no longer hiding behind the mask. Despite all we went through, by the grace of the God, thirty-two years we are still standing. Remember this, your **comeback is always stronger than the setback**. Through this journey my laughter has been restored, my self-esteem resurfaced, blessed, grateful, free, fierce, fabulous and living my best life. It is so true that love conquers all.

I Corinthians 13:4-7 (NIV) ~ "4 Love is patient, love is kind, it does not boast, it is not proud. 5 It does not dishonor others, it is not self-seeking, it is not easily angered, it keeps no record of wrongs. 6 Love does not delight in evil but rejoices with the truth. 7 It always protects, always trust, always hopes, always perseveres."

Yes, we have been married for thirty-two years and still standing walking as a billboard as to what God can do in your life if you just trust him. If you just trust him, he will restore and give all back if not more.

"True freedom comes when you remove your masks."

"All of the best love stories have one thing in

common, you have to go against

the odds to get there.

The couples that are 'Meant To Be' are the ones

who go through everything that's designed to

tear them apart and come out even 'Stronger.' "

***

Tarralyn Jones

"In society, we are faced with various pressures like lifestyle, social media acceptance, appearance, secrets, embedded hurts, etc. that lead you to wearing a mask to conceal who you really are."

Chapter Thirteen

It's Time To Identify The Mask You Are Wearing

I t's time to identify your mask and take the necessary steps to remove this smothering mask so you can live your best life. This act is becoming the norm for many women in today's society. This chosen lifestyle has defined your happiness, acceptance, and comfort state. In society, we are faced with various pressures like lifestyle, social media acceptance, appearance, secrets, embedded hurts, etc. that lead you to wearing a mask to conceal who you really are.

Are you the woman who everyone thinks has an ideal marriage? You have all the material things others may desire such as the home, car, jewelry, children, husband, etc. But behind closed doors your home is in turmoil. You've chosen to remain and deal with the craziness only to have the so call luxuries as well as the man you feel others desire to have for social reasons.

Are you the woman that is sleeping with the enemy? He is your husband but secretly vindictive and conniving. He tends to manipulate and poison everyone's perception of you, he in the eyes of your surrounding is the prefect husband and father, his lies has turned everyone against you by making you appear unstable, and convince others you are the one who is unstable as the wife and mother. Now you feel isolated because he has tarnished your creditability and everyone believes him and not you.

Are you the woman that you and husband involved in the ministry with the added pressures of your leadership role? Behind closed doors you are living in a life of misery. Experiencing no communication, he tends to be more attentive to the needs of others than his own household. This action has caused a separation among your children, yourself and husband. At this point you are feeling a form of loneliness and contemplating to leave the situation but due to the vested time you've put in the marriage, church, and family you've decided to remain.

Are you the woman living with a "functional addict?" A functional addict is defined as a person who appear normal but are under some form of influence whether it is alcohol, drugs, porn, etc. that has gone undetected among his peers. This action can go undetected to the outsiders but you are forced to deal with the issues at hand resulting in life ruin consequences.

Are you the woman dealing with infidelities & promiscuous behavior? He constantly blames you or simply denies his actions. You have tried to compete with his comparisons of other women but always fail with his brutal verbal attacks.

You try to meet his needs with exhaustion and the end result is more verbal attacks. You are finding yourself not confident as to who you are by developing low self-esteem. This view of yourself has caused you to compare your insecurities to other women. You have tried to appease him in many ways finding yourself settling and accepting his behavior only to remain with him despite his actions.

Are you the woman that has a successful career and dealing with a jealousy? This companion is always criticizing you resulting to lessening your confidence in your successes and abilities. Also, experiencing he is validating his actions by continuously saying negative things around your family and friends directed towards you. This method of abuse is an old term called "brow-beating." Simply making you feel less than who you really are as a control mechanism.

Are you the woman who cannot communicate with your companion because everything you say or do is constantly challenged? Never once has given an encouraging word or support. This individual is constantly making brutal comments to discredit everything you say or do. Also, making you feel your communication is lacking and not clear. This is a form of attacking your self-esteem making you feel you are not up to their level of others.

Are you the woman who is the bread winner in your home while the other party sits and not contribute to any responsibilities in the home? When the topic is presented the results are either verbal or physical abuse. Sometimes simply watches you maintain the financial responsibility of the home with resulting in the other party either not working or hardly working.

Are you the woman who has experienced someone simply walk out of your life with no apparent reason or indicated he no longer wants to be with you? This action causes a sense of abandonment and left you in dismay, inability to trust or tendency to sabotage new relationships.

Are you the woman who was experiencing medical issues during the course of your relationship and notice there is no moral support instead he has become a stranger by his actions and responses leaving you with a feeling of betrayal and loneliness.

Are you the woman who experienced your husband taking advantage of you financially. Someone you trusted with an idea of building a future together. He has ruined your credit by exhausting your financial resources, etc. The end result is a sense of loss and difficult time recovering.

Are you the woman who is living in a house and one minute he is loving you and the next minute he is hating you? You've become confused by his actions. You have realized he is a manipulator playing a role for survival to simply remain in the home for convenience.

Are you the woman who has been involved in several relationships but has not had one to commit? Just when you feel a commitment has been established, later find out he simply do not want to marry simply desire to keep you only as a convenience, side piece, or no intentions to commit.

Are you the woman that has managed your religion, career, and finances well? In the eyes of your peers you are considered the "good church girl," but has found you are the conversation piece among your peers and others. Questioning why are you not married? You are feeling a sense of loneliness or depression because there is no candidate in sight. You are asking God several questions such as, "What is wrong with me? Why are other women getting married and not me? Why hasn't anyone pursued me?" Now you are settling in your thought process, you will never get married causing unbearable deep somatic pain.

Are you the single parent that is focused on survival for you and your children? You are being approached by either married men or men that do not have your best interest at heart.

Because they think you are easy access due to your current state and the impression of apparent desperation for someone in your life to care and assist with financial responsibilities. You are now feeling the sense of hopelessness.

Are you the woman who is married to a man that you deny not true to his preferred sexuality? Instead, you are willing to remain in the relationship for social status, convenience and subconsciously thinking you can change him.

Are you the woman who hides your insecurities behind an established relationship that maliciously removes anyone or anything taking away attention or focus on you?

Are you the woman who had lonely childhood due to parents focused on providing all of the material things of life but no personal time? It has resulted in you feeling a void in your life that has caused you to seek attention or wrong choices to fulfill the void.

Are you the woman who has been sworn to silence of your affair that resulted to having a child out of wedlock? You are convinced not to reveal who the father is for the exchange of taking care of you and the child needs with additional promises, or simply left to bear the criticism alone.

Are you the woman who was raped by your stepfather, father, friend, co-worker, relative, or a stranger? There are reoccurrences of the event(s) in your dreams, daily walk or reminders. In some cases, you are constantly reminded due to the attacker being in your midst and never identified by you the victim. You have learned to suppress your feelings only to avoid the pain so you can live a normal life. There is no normal life because it has turned to a continuous nightmare that has left you with embedded internal scars that are left untreated.

Are you the woman who has remarried and realized you have made a grave mistake by marrying for the wrong reasons and found he is not the right mate for you? This person has been identified as a wolf in sheep's clothing. You are now feeling your relationship is in a web of entanglement. Leaving you feeling in a mode of depression, betrayal, and sense of embarrassment for not identifying this person as to whom he really is.

Are you the woman who is a faithful church goer and dealing with turmoil in the home? You are dealing with an unbeliever and makes your life as a Christian quite difficult by constantly testing your beliefs. In some cases, you are accused of allocating too much time in the church and making you feel uncomfortable with your Christian values in the home.

Are you the woman who has a controlling environment? This person retrieves all of your mail, phone calls, emails, etc. Even randomly becomes involved in your daily routine involving friends and family, only to make sure you are not too comfortable in a setting away from your home. In even in some cases deliberately drives you to and from your destinations as a control method to see who you interact with. When you attend functions, you are not allowed to indulge in conversation or mingle with others, only to attend and leave immediately thereafter.

Are you the woman who has so many internal mishaps until you feel you are not good enough for anyone to marry? You have a past that is very dark and feels it can never be revealed. Why?

Because you feel if anyone found out about your past, they will treat you differently or lose respect for you. This has left you believing and feeling tarnished.

Are you the woman that has been living or desire the lifestyle that will not be acceptable to your family, colleague, and friends. Therefore, you have chosen to live your lifestyle in secret.

Are you the woman that is living in a dangerous setting which involved several threatening remarks toward your life? You are afraid and carefully planning an escape. The plan to escape has caused great fear because it may bring harm to you and your family. So now your escape plan has come to a halt only to continue the acceptance of the threats to save others.

Are you the woman who contracted a disease whether by infidelities or your promiscuous acts? It has caused you to feel a sense that your life is ruined and considered damaged goods.

Are you the woman who has lost someone that played an integral part in your life? When that person has transitioned and no longer here, resulted in you feeling lost and alone.

Are you the woman that has a hidden drug or alcohol problem? This act has become a part of your life in order to function? This has resulted in a series of events in your life that has left you mentally handicap without the use of drug or alcohol.

Are you the woman that enjoyed causing pain to others as the mistress or simply being vindictive because of your relationship with married men or someone that is knowingly committed to someone else other than you resulting in you indulging in sexual acts to receive monetary gifts, secret getaway trips, accompany him on business trips, living arrangements, etc.? Because of your acts, you are being haunted in your mindset, but you are not willing to give up the life-style of convenience or "kept woman."

Are you the woman who loves attention and will do in and everything to obtain that personal focus on oneself? You are finding yourself dressing provocatively, making yourself available to the highest bidder, etc. Any act to make you feel the center of attention. This act is leading you to a road of destruction but the hunger for attention outweighs the results of destruction.

Are you the woman who is considered attractive but cannot overcome low self-esteem because of many regrets in your life? Regrets that keep resurfacing in every thought pattern you can't seem to overcome.

Are you the woman that secretly desires more material possessions than her peers? Finding if your peers began to have more than you, you began to secretly become jealous and a need to always be on top despite the cost. Your behavior of secret greed has found and competition is a replacement of the emptiness in your life resulting to a life of misery.

Are you this woman who is caught up in this social media platform masking who you are or presenting yourself as a mystery to engage followers? By engaging followers have become satisfaction of acceptance.

Are you a woman caught up in a web of confusion? This confusion can be with your family, friends or colleagues that has hindered your blessings and growth. I Corinthians 14:33 – "For God is not the author of confusion, but of peace, as in all churches of the saints."

Are you the woman who has been battling personal insecurities that has caused you to divulge in food which resulted in gaining a tremendous amount of weight simply losing yourself in a form of depression and dislike to who you have become.

Are you the woman who has found yourself drinking just to help you deal with the pain and pressure you are experiencing in your life? Only now you find you have become a bonafide alcoholic.

Are you the woman who has made grave mistakes when the pressures became too great to survive? These decisions resulted in dealing with legal repercussions and/or jail.

Are you the woman who has found yourself desiring or having cosmetic surgery to face and body just to feel confident not just for yourself but to appease the person you are in a relationship with or others? Maybe you've found all the cosmetic enhancements still left you dealing with a void in your life.

Have you identified or can relate to one of these women? Are you "Living A Masked Life?" All of us has experienced a form of a personal battle(s) in our lives. You see, the enemy loves to have you restricted, not loving you and refraining you from living your best life.

This is my time to let women know to "live, laugh, love," use your gifts and talents to help others, become an advocate for what you believe in, instill in each other how to be a strong, determined, independent women who loves themselves first. Empower one another with support and love steering away from that dreadful "Jealous" spirit. Share your successes and failures that can encourage others. Make an emphasis on someone life by always putting God first in your life for direction. Also continuing to love yourself first, and this action will prevent you from living behind a mask.

*It's Time To Identify The Mask
You Are Wearing*

"Life is like a roller coaster. You can either scream every time there is a bump or you can throw your hands up and enjoy the ride."

***

Tarralyn Jones

"Take care of yourself, mind-body-soul. You are the "PRIORITY!" I am tired of women simply settling and allowing wearing a mask to steal your joy, peace and identity."

Chapter Fourteen

Steps In Removing The Mask

Wearing a mask strips away years of your life, joy, peace, and happiness. Are you ready to remove this mask that has held you hostage? Hopefully, the answer is "YES." Let's take these steps together in removing your mask.

1 John 3:8 (KJV) - He that committeth sin is of the devil; for the devil sinneth from the beginning. For this purpose the Son of God was manifested, that he might destroy the works of the devil.

The Son of God unties people from all kinds of the works of the devil, untangling Satan's hold on them just as this mask is doing to you.

2 Corinthians 10:4 - (KJV) - For the weapons of our warfare are not carnal, but mighty through God to the pulling down of strong holds.

You see the mind is the prime location the devil attacks. He identifies where he can be successful in planting a stronghold of deception in your mind then he can control and manipulate. Are you getting any closer to removing this mask you are wearing? I pray you are. If you are still concealing and hiding you won't be able to heal.

I know you are desiring to have that yearning peace of mind. You need to understand what peace means and how it feels. Peace is freedom, living in harmony, live without fear and having the freedom to fully be yourself. You don't make any comparisons or questioning if you should have done this or that, and not measuring your success or failures with material things or others. Having happiness and a peace of mind is what make your life successful. I love this quote by I love this quote by Albert Einstein: "Peace of mind transpires and thrives when you let go of the things that limit your growth and happiness."

Second, you will experience the most precious word, "Joy." This reminds me of this song I Love by the great Shirley Caesar, "This joy that I have, the world didn't give to me, this joy that I have, the world didn't give it to me, the world didn't give it, the world can't take it away."

I want you to read this paragraph very carefully.

Take care of yourself, mind-body-soul. You are the "PRIORITY!" I am tired of women simply settling and allowing wearing a mask to steal your joy, peace and identity. "STOP" educate yourself on things you are unsure of, find resources to manifest that dream of yours, be persistent in turning the impossibilities into reality, do not neglect your health needs, listen to your body because you have an internal indicator, you just have to listen and pay close attention. Remember there is no perfect person, everyone has made mistakes, have regrets, or have experience personal battles. Learn to beautify yourself gracefully both internal and external. Although you may not feel like it, step out everyday with an attitude of accomplishment and confidence looking and acting like you own the world.

"STOP" having an untidy appearance whenever you are not feeling your best or simply just going through. Leave your home looking revived, refreshed, renewed, rejuvenated, as a woman that has it all together. Don't get caught looking busted and disgusted. This is what the enemy desire you to look, just like what you are going through. You stand flat-footed and let the enemy know, "I will look good swinging and will look good winning!" Change the Game!

"Are you ready to say, Lord here I am? I need you, Lord, to help me realize if I am wearing a mask. Don't turn to your left or right but keep your eyes focused on healing and deliverance..."

Chapter Fifteen

Healing and Deliverance

I have shared with you how I became the woman with the mask by being transparent in sharing my story and the scenario of other women identifying if you too are hiding and living behind a mask. We are survivors, we know how to endure pain without the pain effecting our role in life only to make us stronger. II Timothy 2:3 (KJV) says, "Thou therefore endure hardness, as a good soldier of Jesus Christ." This simply means when your trials increase, you need to grow stronger, your faith increases, and your love for Christ becomes stronger. This mask has you feeling smothered and off balance resulted in distracted, encountering road blocks in your path, vision distorted, success hindered, all becoming an emotional roller coaster. Remember if you patiently trust in God's plan and use adversity to grow stronger, the trials of life will ultimately lead to joy.

I am often reminded about a wise woman who shared a story with me years ago as a young woman to enjoy life and take care of yourself. I remembered asking. Why? Her response was if you are dealing with everybody problems and situations, etc. and end up getting sick and possibly death. Guess what? Funeral arrangements will take place, they will grieve, funeral will take place, people will have nice things to say about you, funeral will be over, then everyone heads to the grave site to bury you, family and friends gravitate back for the repast, then everyone leaves and go back to their individual homes and lives. Now you are just a memory. Let Go, Let God, & Live your Best Life!

Let's begin taking the necessary steps to removing this mask that has consumed your life.

Are you ready to say, Lord here I am? I need you, Lord, to help me realize if I am wearing a mask. Don't turn to your left or right but keep your eyes focused on healing and deliverance asking the Lord for forgiveness repenting casting away the things of the old with trusting the father for the new way of life and that is trusting him in your daily walk.

Place your hand on your face to lift the mask. Come on, you can do it in Jesus name! Close your eyes and lift the mask. Do you feel the mask being lifted spiritually? There it is in the center of your face, almost there don't stop! While you are lifting the mask, just say to yourself, "I am Healed, Delivered, And Set Free, In Jesus Name." Keep saying those words while you are lifting the mask across your face. Almost there, the mask is lifted pass the center of your face. You are starting to feel a breath of fresh air, your vision is clearer, you don't sound muzzled or feel smothered. Keep lifting, the mask, it is almost off. Keep repeating, "I am Healed, Delivered, And Set Free, In Jesus Name." You are starting to feel your deliverance, a weight has been lifted, your mind is no longer clouded. Thank the Lord you have completed the task, the mask is off. Praise God! Take that mask and stomp on it, letting the devil know that you have the victory. You no longer living a masked life.

Now you can raise your hands and say authoritatively, "I AM HEALED, DELIVERED, AND SET FREE!"

This has been a joyous experience writing about my walk in life living a mask life. I am even more overjoyed to assist you in recognizing if you are wearing a mask, identifying your mask, and steps in removing the mask towards being delivered and set free.

1 Corinthians 15:57 (KJV) says, "But thanks be to God, which giveth us the victory through our Lord Jesus Christ."

You must remember throughout the Bible, you see the rewards of those who overcame their trials, who stood firm, and keep the devil in his place. God gave us the victory. So walk like you are victorious!

Group Discussion & Questions

1. In reading *Living A Masked Life*, were there a mask you can relate with that you are wearing. Can you determine how you became the person in wearing the mask?

2. Did you find comfort in hiding behind a mask? Why?

3. Do you find in today's society wearing a mask has become the "NORM" & Why? Expound on the reason.

4. Social media is an undeniable force in modern society, do you feel this new wave of expression has contributed to living a masked life for acceptance? Discuss.

5. Why you rather live a masquerade behind the mask hiding your true self?

6. If you identified a mask you are wearing, have you taken the necessary steps in the removal of the mask?

7. Do you find yourself struggling to remove the mask? Discuss.

8. In the removal of the mask, how does it feel to no longer be in bondage to the world's expectations.

Reflections

About The Author

Tarralyn Jones, Founder & Principal of TJ's Designs & Events serves as the leading force of boutique firm and a force to reckon with in her God-given talent of creating custom and stunning creations. Before crossing the pond to the special events & design market, she was once an executive and director in the healthcare administration and medical field for over a decade. After willingly planning galas and corporate functions on the side, she realized her heart was set on becoming a professional event strategist, which in 2004 lead to the formation of TJ's Promotions & Event Planning. Not only is she dedicated to special events & design, but is also a devoted philanthropist, having served on the board for Kids Beating Cancer, Florida Hospital Cancer Institute, Business & Professional Women's Federation (Former-President), Business & the National Association For Female Executives. Tarralyn is also known for her calling and work as an Evangelist Missionary.

Tarralyn is a two-time breast cancer survivor and years later had two tumors removed from her brain. As a result of enduring these life-changing experiences, she currently takes an active role in Breast Cancer and /Brain Tumor Awareness month every year.

A die hard Seminole, Tarralyn pursued her undergraduate studies in Business Administration at Florida State University, and completed the Supervisory Leadership Certification Program at Rollins College. Tarralyn is the devoted wife to Willie Jones Sr, and mother of three beautiful children

About The Author

Brian, Candace, & Christian. Tarralyn is a devoted advocate passionate about inspiring, motivating, and educating women to live, laugh, love and be a self-love diva. Tarralyn loves creating platforms and planning events to encourage and pour into the hearts of hurting women. In her private time she enjoys daily meditation with the Lord, decorating, reading, travel, and spending quality time with her family.

Contact The Author

You are welcome to email or write the author with comments about this book. You are also welcome to contact her for bookings. Tarralyn is available for book club presentations, book signings, or speaking engagements for your group or organization (conferences, workshops, retreats, seminars, women's groups, women's ministries and women's clubs).

Contact her at:

www.tarralynjones.com

Email:
author@tarralynjones.com

Connect with her on social media:

Facebook:
Tarralyn Callins-Jones
https://www.facebook.com/tarralyn.jones

Instagram:
Tarralyn Jones @tarrajones1
https://www.instagram.com/tarrajones1

Twitter:
Tarralyn Jones @Tarrajones1
https://twitter.com/tarrajones1